PEOPLES AND THEIR ENVIRONMENTS™

PEOPLES OF THE RAIN FOREST

Robert Low

The Rosen Publishing Group's
PowerKids Press™
New York

Published in 1996 by The Rosen Publishing Group, Inc.
29 East 21st Street, New York, NY 10010

First Edition

Book design: Kim Sonsky

Photo credits: Cover © Eliot Elisofon/Eliot Elisofon Photographic Archives, National Museum of African Art, Smithsonian Institution; pp. 4, 12, 20 © Bertrand Rieger/Gamma Liaison; p. 7 © Wendy Stone/Gamma Liaison; pp. 8, 15 © Dr. Colin M. Turnbull, Joseph Allen Towles Collection, Avery Research Center for African American History & Culture; p. 11 © Pat Zelt/ANAKO Editions; p. 16 © Pacific Pictures–John Penisten/Liaison International; p. 19 © Lam Duc/ANAKO Editions.

Low, Robert, 1952–
    Peoples of the rain forest / Robert Low.
          p.   cm. — (Peoples and their environments)
    Includes index.
    Summary: Describes life in the rain forests of the world and how people survive there.
    ISBN 0-8239-2297-9
    1. Human geography—Tropics—Juvenile literature. 2. Rain forests—Juvenile literature.
  [1. Human geography—Tropics. 2. Rain forests.] I. Title. II. Series: Low, Robert, 1952–
  GF895.L69 1996
  304.2′3′09152—dc20   96-5551
                                                             CIP
                                                                AC

Manufactured in the United States of America

CONTENTS

What Is a Rain Forest?

A rain forest is a forest in an area that receives lots of rain each year. There are rain forests in many places in the world. Most rain forests grow in **tropical** (TROP-i-kul) areas.

Trees in rain forests grow so close together that their leaves let only a little light through. Even so, bushes and plants live beneath the branches. The rain forest is rich with plant and animal life.

◀ Rain forests are filled with a wide variety of trees and plants.

Peoples of the Rain Forest

Many different peoples live in rain forests all over the world. For example, the **Mbuti** (mm-BOO-tee) live in the **Ituri** (ee-TUR-ee) rain forest in Africa. The **Huaorani** (hoo-RON-ee) live in the **Amazon** (AM-uh-zon) rain forest in South America. And the **Dayak** (DY-ak) live in a rain forest on **Borneo** (BORE-nee-oh), an island near Asia.

These peoples live in different places and speak different languages. But because they live in rain forests, they have many things in common.

The Mbuti are one of many peoples who live in the Ituri rain forest. ▶

LIVING IN THE RAIN FOREST

Many people who live in rain forests move from place to place to hunt and grow food. When they move to a new place, the people cut down trees and burn them. The smoke and ash carry **nutrients** (NOO-tree-entz) from the trees to the soil. Then there is enough healthy soil and sunlight to grow more food.

Many peoples who live in the rain forest hunt the animals who live there. The Mbuti hunt with spears and nets. The Huaorani use blowguns.

◄ The Mbuti hunt with bows and arrows, as well as spears and nets.

Animals and Plants

The rain forest is home to many animals, from the birds and monkeys that live in the treetops to snakes and insects that crawl along the ground. The Ituri rain forest, home to the Mbuti, is also home to elephants and gorillas. Wild pigs live in the Amazon, where the Huaorani live. And the Dayak share the island of Borneo with rhinoceros and deer.

Some of the plants in rain forests help people get well when they are sick. Others are good for food. Still others are **poisonous** (POY-zun-us).

The Huaorani share the Amazon rain forest with brightly colored parrots. ▶

Traveling in Rain Forests

Many people walk through the rain forests, cutting trails as they go. However, cutting a trail through the rain forest is hard work, and the plants grow back quickly. So some people travel on rivers, using **canoes** (kuh-NOOZ) or rafts made of wood.

The Dayak live on an island with many mountains. The trails there are steep and slippery. To cross narrow valleys more easily, the Dayak make bridges out of **bamboo** (bam-BOO). The Dayak also travel on water buffalo.

◀ The Dayak also use canoes to travel on the rivers of Borneo.

Food in the Rain Forest

There are few stores or markets in the rain forests. The people who live there hunt, fish, and farm. The Mbuti use spears, nets, and bows and arrows to hunt. They fish in the rivers. They also eat fruit and nuts that they gather.

The Huaorani make blowguns out of wood. They use the blowguns to blow poisoned darts at the animals they hunt. They also fish and grow **manioc** (MAN-ee-ock) and corn.

The Dayak fish and use blowguns and spears to hunt. They also grow rice on the mountainsides.

The Mbuti eat the food that they hunt and gather in the rain forest. ▶

Clothing

In the tropical rain forests the weather is very warm all year round. There is little need for heavy clothing there. Instead, the Mbuti wear small pieces of clothing made out of flattened tree bark.

Some Huaorani wear a small piece of cloth wrapped around their waists. Most Huaorani children wear no clothes.

The Dayak wear clothes made from cloth that they weave themselves.

◀ The Dayak weave cloth with pretty colors and patterns. The cloth is then made into clothes.

BUILDING HOMES

Because many people who live in the rain forest move often, they live in homes that can be built easily and quickly. The Mbuti make beehive-shaped homes out of wooden poles. These are bent, tied down, and covered with leaves. The Huaorani make their homes out of bamboo poles covered with leaves.

The Dayak stay in one place. They build huge longhouses on stilts. The floors and walls are made of bamboo or tree bark. The roofs are made of **thatched** (THACHT) palm leaves.

Huaorani homes are made from bamboo poles and leaves. ▶

Families and Communities

The Mbuti live in groups of 10 to 25 families. They help each other find food and build homes. About once a month, the groups move to a new area in the Ituri rain forest.

Huaorani families usually live alone, far apart from each other. Each family moves in search of new, fresh soil in which to plant a garden.

The Dayak live in settled villages. There are several longhouses in each village. As many as 50 or more Dayak families live in a longhouse. The villagers work together to hunt, grow rice, and run the village.

◀ The Dayak show pride in their culture by wearing colorful traditional clothing for a celebration.

Challenges of the Rain Forest

Today, the people who live in the rain forests face new challenges. Many rain forests are being destroyed by people who do not live there. These people sell wood, oil, and rubber from the rain forests. They tear down trees to start big farms or cattle ranches. Now it is harder for the Mbuti to find animals to hunt and for the Huaorani to find places to grow food. Their rain forests are getting smaller. Many Dayak still live much as they always have. But they, too, now share the mountains in their rain forest with others who live differently.

Glossary

Amazon (AM-uh-zon) rain forest Rain forest in South America.

bamboo (bam-BOO) A large, tree-like plant, with a strong, hollow stem.

Borneo (BORE-nee-oh) Island near the coast of Asia.

canoe (kuh-NOO) Narrow boat made out of wood.

Dayak (DY-ak) A people who live in the mountainous rain forest of Borneo.

Huaorani (hoo-RON-ee) A people who live in the Amazon rain forest of South America.

Ituri (ee-TUR-ee) rain forest Rain forest in central Africa.

manioc (MAN-ee-ok) Plant whose roots are used for food.

Mbuti (mm-BOO-tee) A people who live in the Ituri rain forest in Africa.

nutrient (NOO-tree-ent) Something that helps plants or animals grow bigger, stronger, or healthier.

poison (POY-zun) Substance that can hurt or kill a living being.

thatch (THACH) To put grass or leaves together tightly to make a roof.

tropical (TROP-i-kul) Describes the part of the world that is warm all year round.

INDEX